DEAD SICK
Incredible Medicine from History

Coming Back to Life

Some people think history is dead and buried. It happened so long ago, it must be dead dull. Right? Wrong! The past never really goes away. Why? Because historical stories can live on for ages. What's more, they can be dead amazing!

So how exactly does the past stay with us? Well, it all begins with authors today who have a thirst for knowledge. They find out about the past from old pictures, buildings and texts, then they turn all this information into stories in books. You read the books and – hey presto – the past comes right back to life!

This is one of those books. It's full of dead interesting and sometimes dead gruesome stories about the past. Just turn the page and see for yourself …

Contents

If you're squeamish, you might want to look away now! This book is all about fighting to stay alive. It describes how our **ancestors** have battled through the years to overcome sickness and disease. Sometimes the cures were dead weird and sometimes they were just dead sick. Let's have a look at some of the gruesome things doctors used to do to their patients in the past, all in the name of medicine!

Chapter 1
The Unseen Enemy

Why do I feel so sick?

Until quite recent times, the world was a dead sick place. In fact, people found it pretty hard just staying alive. They suffered wounds that couldn't be healed and caught diseases that couldn't be cured. So why didn't they just go to the doctor for help?

Well, for three reasons:

1. There were far fewer doctors in the past.
2. Doctors often didn't know how to make people better because they didn't know why people got ill in the first place.
3. People usually had to pay for medical treatment so only the rich could afford to see the doctor!

I'll take your money. But I don't have a clue what's wrong with you!

Why Were the Doctors in the Dark?

One way of finding out how something works – and why it isn't working – is to look at it very closely. Yet doctors in the past didn't observe or examine their patients like they do today. Amazing as it seems, they just used to guess what might be wrong.

Ah, you have a pain in your head? An evil spirit must have got in there!

This wasn't really medicine – it was **superstition**. As time went by, doctors grew less superstitious and relied more on observation. They still had one small problem though: things they couldn't see were making people sick. Who were these mysterious enemies?

Germs! Throughout history germs have made people sick and even killed them. But for a long time, doctors didn't even know that they existed. So with very little knowledge, how did doctors treat their patients in the past?

Chapter 2
Spells and Prayers

4000-7000 years ago

Now that's what I call magic!

In ancient times, people blamed angry gods and demons for their **ailments**. Medicine and religion were very closely linked together. Doctors were more like **priests** asking gods to cure their patients.

A 'Hole' Lot of Pain

What would you prefer: a headache or a hole in the head? In ancient times it could be a straight choice! People believed headaches were caused by evil spirits. They believed these spirits could be driven out by 'trepanning' – that's having holes scraped in their skulls!

Believe it or not, people actually survived this early form of brain surgery. Some even went back for more! We know this because ancient skulls have been found with several holes in them. The bone had carried on growing for a little while after it had been cut, showing that the treatment was given to *living* people!

You nearly forgot your regular trepanning appointment!

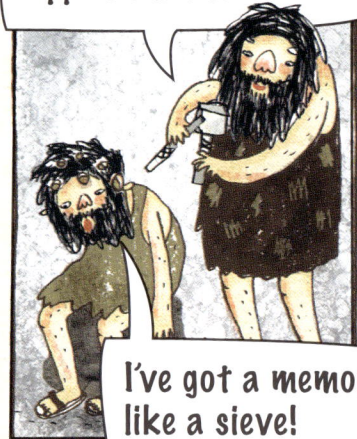

I've got a memory like a sieve!

Gods to the Rescue

One place that seemed particularly full of spiteful spirits and gods was Ancient Egypt. Egyptian doctors believed these spirits caused people to get gruesomely sick.

So what was the solution? Well, only a really terrible treatment would drive them away ...

Ancient Egyptian Cures

Sore, stinging eye? There's only one solution ...

- Take a tortoise's brain and mash it up.
- Mix the mash with honey so it gets extra gooey.
- Place the mixture on the eye.
- Pray to Isis, the goddess of healing, for help.

This had better work!

The most important part of this treatment – or magical spell – was the prayer to the goddess. For while Egyptians believed horrible gods could make them sick, they thought *friendly* gods could cure them.

Charming!

Doctors felt sure a bird-like god called Horus could keep them fit and well. So rich Egyptians often had a protecting 'Eye of Horus' painted on their jewellery.

The little hippo charm or 'amulet' on the right was meant to do a similar kind of job. A pregnant woman would have worn the amulet, representing the goddess Tawaret, to keep evil spirits from harming her unborn child. Look closely. The goddess is pregnant too!

If you were unlucky enough to have lots of problems, you'd need a special amulet ...

Do I look scary enough?

This will scare off all the disease-demons.

(eye) infection caused by flies and desert sand

(skull) small holes caused by lack of iron in diet

(gut) parasite eggs swallowed in water from Nile river

(teeth) badly worn from eating gritty bread

(lungs) pneumonia caused by breathing in desert sand

Jobs for the Girls

The doctor on the last page was a man – like most doctors in history. But, unusually, in Egypt women could also be treated by female healers. They were called 'swnwts'. Try saying that with a mouthful of sand!

Surprising Successes

So, was all ancient medicine superstitious nonsense relying on the power of unseen gods and goddesses? Not exactly. Look at this list of items. They were part of ancient medical kits – and they worked!

- Bone needles and animal **sinew**: to stitch up wounds.
- Giant ants: to clamp wounds together with their jaws. When you twisted off the ant's head, the jaws stayed in place!
- Clay: to make **casts** for broken bones.
- Herbs: to soothe stomach ache, fever and battle wounds.

The very earliest doctors *did* have some useful treatments, but they didn't really understand how the body worked. Then along came some Ancient Greeks who decided they had the answers ...

Chapter 3
Seeing the Humour

2000-3000 years ago

Good sense of humours? That's me!

Ancient Greece and Ancient Rome were full of extremely clever people. **Pioneer** doctors like Greek Hippocrates (say: *Hip-oc-ra-tees*) and Roman Galen (say: *Gay-len*) helped make medicine less religious. But they still had an awful lot to learn.

Dream Cures

The Ancient Greeks, like the Ancient Egyptians, were big fans of religious medicine. The top Greek doctor-god was called Asclepius (say: *as-cleep-ee-us*). If you were sick, you didn't go to his surgery – you went to one of his temples!

This 2300-year-old carving shows a sick Greek woman asleep in a temple of Asclepius. Greek doctors believed that Asclepius would visit patients in their dreams and cure them.

The Healing Tree

Not *all* Greek doctors had such magical ideas about medicine though. A doctor called Hippocrates came up with some top treatments of his own.

One of his treatments is still around today. He found that parts of the willow tree could be used as a painkiller. We now call this painkiller 'Aspirin'.

But Hippocrates was on the wrong track elsewhere ...

So Hippocrates wasn't – ahem – barking up the wrong tree!

A Question of Balance

Q. Did you hear about the man who got a pain in his eye whenever he drank coffee?

A. The doctor told him to take the spoon out. Ha ha!

OK, so that's a bad joke, but we bet it made you laugh. And we all know humour makes you feel better. So why did the great Hippocrates believe humours made you sick? Well firstly, he was talking about humour**s**, notice – with an 's'. So what were they?

Hippocrates' Guide to Humours

Humours are important liquids inside the body.
There are four types:

Blood: hot and wet and gives you energy
Phlegm (snot): cold and wet and helps you cool down
Yellow bile: hot and dry and helps you digest food
Black bile: cold and dry and – er – a bit mysterious
(but you definitely need it!).

When there are just the right amounts of all four humours
inside you, you stay healthy. But if you have too much of
any one humour, things start to go wrong.

Problem: Too much black bile, leading to **depression.**
Solution: Drain the black bile by cutting the skin and
letting the patient bleed.

**My treatments
are guaranteed to
keep you well and
balanced.**

I think I preferred being depressed.

Although Hippocrates was wrong about what caused
sickness, he *did* know gods and spirits weren't to blame.

Seeing is Believing

Hippocrates said that careful observation was the first step in treating a patient. More than 500 years later, another pioneering doctor agreed.

Galen worked in Ancient Rome studying and treating the wounds of gladiators. The gladiators thrilled crowds by fighting wild beasts and each other – often to the death. So you can imagine the injuries Galen had to treat!

But Galen wanted to get an even better idea of how the body worked. How? By cutting up the corpses of dead gladiators. This was against the law, so he had to cut up animals instead.

Now if you were a chicken, I'd know exactly how to fix you.

Ancient Greek and Roman doctors seemed to be leaving superstition behind. But history is hardly ever straightforward! More than a thousand years later, magical medicine was back with a bang ...

Chapter 4
Faith Healing
600-900 years ago

One touch from me is all it takes!

The medieval world was riddled with disease, yet few doctors knew how to fight it. Some doctors in non-Christian countries continued with Galen's hands-on approach. But in Europe's Christian countries, people looked to their God to heal them.

It's a Miracle!

Like the Ancient Greeks, Medieval Christians also prayed for miracle cures. Unlike the Greeks, they didn't always expect their God to heal them in person. They believed he worked in more mysterious ways ...

Powder Power!

Feeling a bit under the weather? Nip down to your local **cathedral!** It's God's house so it's full of holy healing power. See all those statues of angels? Chip a tiny bit off one of them, pound it into powder, then use it as medicine! You'll soon feel heavenly!

They might feel better, but I've been defaced!

Magic Touch!

Having trouble with your skin? Nasty boils and lumps all over? You've got scrofula. Hurry along to your local palace today and make an appointment with your king! One royal touch and you'll be

as right as reign!

What a handy cure!

Thousands of Christians queued up at royal courts to be touched. They truly believed kings could channel their God's healing powers. Sometimes they *did* get better. Amazing? Just a touch!

But what happened when *millions* of people fell ill? All the magic in the medieval world couldn't help then.

The Great Mystery Illness

You really wouldn't have wanted to be alive in Europe in the 1300s. Or in Africa or Asia, for that matter. A vile disease called the Black Death was sweeping the world.

Imagine the terror. All around, people were dying hideous deaths. First they got a headache and a fever. Then lumps started to appear on their skin. These lumps grew to the size of oranges and split open. Blood and pus oozed out. Yuck! Finally, black spots covered their bodies. The pain was terrible ... it was a truly gruesome way to die.

No one knew how to stop the Black Death because no one knew how it had started. That didn't stop people making some dead weird suggestions though ...

God is clearly fed up with us and our sinning ways. He's sent this disease to punish us.

I'm not being funny, but this is all about humours. Old Hippocrates was right. We're obviously out of balance!

This trouble began when earthquakes released poisonous fumes into the world.

No one had yet worked out what really made people dead sick. Nor how or why disease spread from person to person. This was because no one had identified the germs which caused these plagues.

While the doctors tried to figure it out, people kept dying. Between 1347 and 1352, the Black Death killed around 25 million people in Europe alone. With the doctors baffled, what did people do?

Well, some people whipped themselves in public. They thought this would show God how sorry they were for sinning, then maybe he would stop punishing them.

I think we're flogging a dead horse here!

But the only true solution was for medicine to get real. Superstitious beliefs didn't die out completely, but slowly medicine did start to get more sensible ...

Chapter 5
Blood Everywhere!
400-500 years ago

Yum, yum!

The belief in humours hung around for *ages*. This wasn't at all funny! But after the year 1500, some pioneers came up with new ideas based on observation and not superstition. Yet, as you will see, not every brainwave led to a breakthrough in medicine …

Gruesome Bloodsuckers

If you could afford to see a doctor in the 1500s, your treatment might have involved some little bloodsuckers! Doctors used leeches to 'bleed' you if your humours were out

Now what seems to be the problem?

That!

of balance. Swollen tonsils? No problem. The doctor tied a silk thread around a leech, then slipped it down your throat to slurp off your extra 'bad blood'.

Hairy Tales

But wait – it got worse. Cures were sometimes carried out by local barbers. Really? Your hairdresser? Some barbers even did operations. They could chop off whole limbs!

Just a little off the side, was it?

No More Boiling Oil

Some of these 'barber-surgeons' were great thinkers too. Ambroise Paré was a brainy French barber-surgeon in the 1500s. He treated badly wounded soldiers on the battlefield – and often had to **amputate** limbs. But Paré didn't just chop limbs off, he

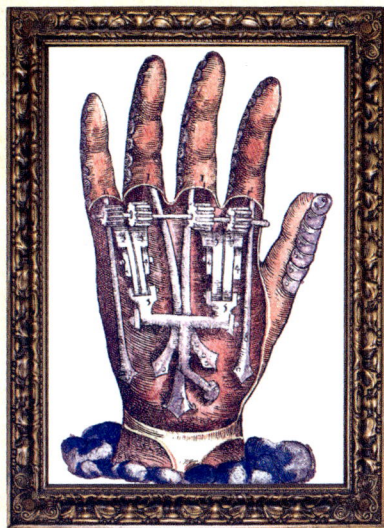

also aimed to replace them! His close study of the human body helped him to find ways to make artificial body parts like the one in the picture.

One of Paré's great brainwaves was to treat wounds in a new way. Traditionally, boiling oil was poured on wounds to kill infections. Ouch! Instead, Paré discovered an **antiseptic ointment** made from egg yolks, oil from roses (unheated!) and **turpentine**. It didn't smell very nice but it worked a treat and was much less painful!

It Sounds Crazy But It Just Might Work

Not every new idea was a good one. In the 1600s, Englishman Kenelm Digby wrote a bestselling book about a wacky 'weapon ointment'. It really is hard to believe ...

Wicked Wounds?

Having trouble healing a nasty sword wound? Follow my directions to make a simple ointment.

You will need:

- worms
- pigs' brains
- powdered human corpse.

He'll be up and about in no time.

Now for the amazing bit! Put the ointment on the sword that caused the wound! Even if the victim is now miles away, his wound will be cured. Amazing or what?

That sounds as if it couldn't possibly work – and it didn't! However, other ideas could *sound* just as crazy but they *did* actually work ...

Until the 1600s, doctors thought blood was gradually 'used up' in human bodies, then more blood was somehow created. But Englishman William Harvey had other ideas. He suggested the same blood kept going round and round. It sounded crazy at the time – but he was right!

Micro Acrobats

In 1683, Dutchman Antony van Leeuwenhoek, made an amazing discovery. One day, after dinner, he scraped his teeth. He studied the white gunk under a microscope – and found curved little creatures tumbling about like acrobats. They were germs and he was the first person ever to see them!

But it was one thing to see germs. It was another to work out what harm they could do.

Medicine had come a long way since the days of temple gods and wacky ointments. But there was still a long way to go. Those pesky little germs had to be figured out for a start ...

Chapter 6
Medicine Gets Modern
100-200 years ago

Catch me if you can!

Amazing breakthroughs during the 1800s helped make medicine a lot more modern. In the never-ending war on disease, medical pioneers finally put superstition behind them. But first, the doctors had to clean up their act.

A Man's World?

Have you noticed how few women doctors have appeared in this book since Ancient Egyptian times? That's because there were hardly any of them. For centuries women worked as nurses or **midwives**, but doctoring was considered a man's job.

When I grow up I want to be a doctor.

You'll be wanting a beard next!

A Matter of Life and Death

In 1847, at the world's largest **maternity hospital** in Austria, a new problem emerged. In one ward, male student doctors delivered newborn babies and, in another, female student midwives delivered the babies. Yet on one ward many more mothers were dying. Why?

Here's what Dr Ignaz Semmelweis thought:

Wash Your Hands!

It is quite clear that we have a hygiene problem in our hospitals. I believe that student doctors are infecting their patients.

I have observed that doctors examine dead patients as well as living ones. Midwives, on the other hand, only treat the living — and far fewer patients die on their wards. All the evidence suggests that the doctors must be **contaminating** their living patients.

We cannot allow this to continue. There is no doubt in my mind that doctors must clean up their act. All doctors must wash their hands with **disinfectant** before treating patients. This will be a major medical step forward. With one simple act we could save many more patients.

Trust me, I'm a doctor. All this blood and pus shows how experienced I am!

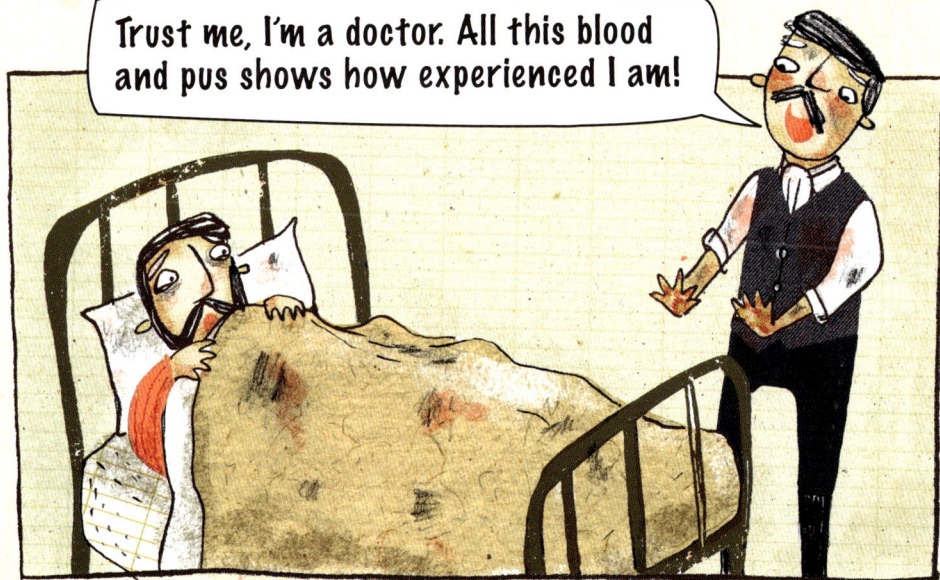

Handwash Hero

It may seem shocking now, but very few experts at the time agreed with Dr Semmelweis. His appeal was largely ignored and he was mocked.

> Hands up if you think Dr Semmelweis is wrong.

This was because people still didn't understand exactly how germs could spread disease. Even Dr Semmelweis was in the dark about that. But he was right about hygiene, and research just a few years later proved it. Hand-washing then became all the rage. And poor old Dr S – now dead himself – was remembered as the 'saviour of mothers'.

War Declared on Germs at Last

For thousands of years germs continued to spread disease, making millions of people sick. But it wasn't until the late 1800s that the war on germs really began.

Frenchman Louis Pasteur and German Robert Koch showed that tiny living microbes are *everywhere*. The word 'microbes' just means 'small lives'. A drop of human spit can hold 40 million microbes – so you can see how small we're talking!

Yet Pasteur and Koch managed to track down a number of disease-causing microbes – or germs. More importantly, they discovered that different germs caused different diseases – from the Black Death right through to measles.

You make me sick!

No, my friend. You make *us* sick.

Now that doctors knew what germs were, they could start to fight them. How?

Well, Pasteur showed how germs made milk go off (and made people who drank it dead sick). But he also found that by heating milk – or 'pasteurising' it – you could kill off all the germs. As with Semmelweis' handwash, *prevention* could be even better than a cure!

Wake Me Up When It's Over

Meanwhile it became much safer to have an operation (in proper hospitals, rather than barber shops). Englishman Joseph Lister pioneered new disinfectants. These were used to keep operating theatres, doctors and patients clean. Germs didn't know what had hit them!

The poor chap below, from the 1790s, had to stay conscious while his leg was being amputated. But in the 1840s, the first patients were given anaesthetic drugs like 'ether' to put them into a pain-free sleep. That was still half a century too late for this chap!

Tell us when it *really* starts to hurt.

By around 1900, medicine had more or less come up to date. Doctors had really started to cure people. So what was left for them to do?

Chapter 7
The War Goes On

Let battle commence.

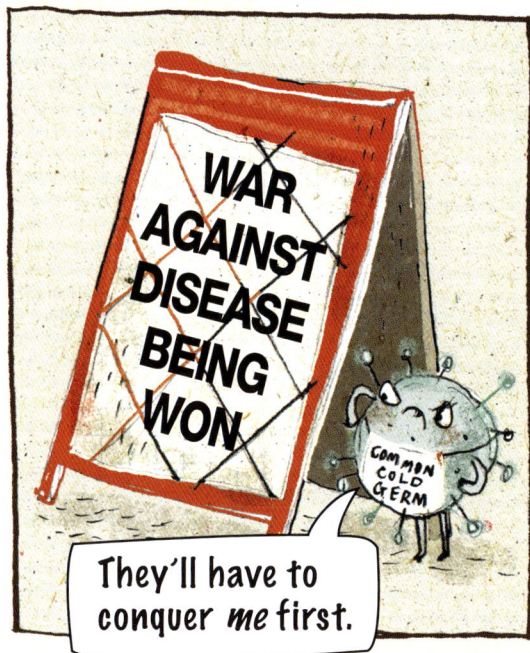

WAR AGAINST DISEASE BEING WON

COMMON COLD GERM

They'll have to conquer *me* first.

Since 1900, doctors have been in a better position than ever to fight sickness. That's great, but one thing they can never do is relax. Just when they might think they've triumphed over disease, a new medical mystery arises.

21st Century Marvellous Medicine

It's amazing how far medicine has come and how quickly it keeps changing. Today, teams of surgeons can transplant hearts and lungs and even give people new faces. We have tiny robots that can crawl through small spaces in our bodies and perform astonishing feats. Our medicine cabinets at home are full of pills and potions. What's more, there are now loads more clued-up doctors than there ever used to be, and in places like Britain they treat their patients free of charge! Sounds fantastic, doesn't it? So what's the problem?

New Challenges, Old Weapons

Germs are clever little enemies. They keep changing. No sooner have doctors worked out ways to defeat them, than the germs work out new ways to stay alive!

There will always be more to understand and more battles to win. Doctors need all the new weapons they can lay their hands on. But sometimes discoveries aren't as new as they seem ...

Sweet Success

Could the war on superbugs be over? These nasty germs have been killing patients in hospitals all over the world.

Experts are amazed that the remedy could be something that has been around for thousands of years – pure and simple honey. "It's killed every kind of germ we've tried it on," said one researcher, buzzing with excitement. "Manuka honey works bee-utifully!" So there you have it, honey isn't just good on toast!

Oh no! It's the Germ-inator!

That's not all. Doctors have been delving back in time to find some truly old ways of doing things ...

Drill Away

Some surgeons now remove bits of their patients' skulls (after an anaesthetic of course!). Not to let evil spirits out – but to reduce pressure on the brain.

Little Suckers

Leeches are making a comeback too. Researchers have found that their saliva fights germs and eases pain.

Docs in Frocks

The battle against germs will always go on. Doctors need all the brainpower they can get. It's great then that since the mid-1800s women doctors have joined the battle. That's when female medical students at last started being trained alongside the men.

I don't like the look of this.

The history of medicine is packed full of dire deeds and terrible treatments. It's enough to make you run for the sick bucket. But it's also full of brilliant minds and truly incredible cures. Who knows what medical mystery will be solved next?

Timeline

Here are some of the doctors and gruesome cures featured in this book:

7000 years ago

2000–3000 years ago

4000 years ago

I've been around forever!

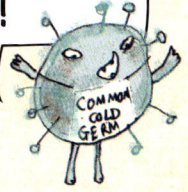

COMMON COLD GERM

400-500 years ago

Now!

600-900 years ago

100-200 years ago

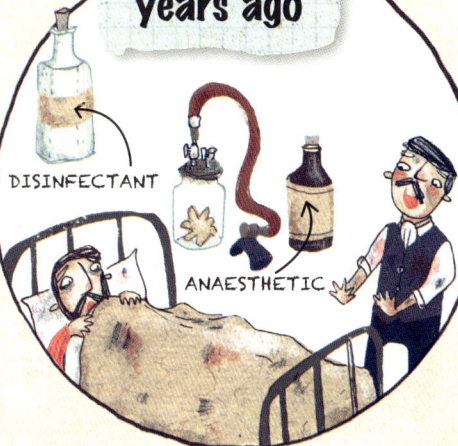

DISINFECTANT

ANAESTHETIC

Glossary

ailments: illnesses

amputate: cut off a part of the body

ancestors: people related to you who lived a long time ago

antiseptic: something that kills germs

casts: stiff cases used to keep broken bones in place

cathedral: large and important church

contaminating: making something dirty by touching it

depression: deep, long-lasting unhappiness

disinfectant: something that kills germs

germs: tiny living things that cause illness

hygiene: cleanliness

iron: metal found in the blood

maternity hospital: where women give birth to their babies

midwives: people who help women when they are giving birth

ointment: soft, oily cream that is rubbed into the skin

parasite: plant or animal that lives on or in another living thing

pioneer: first person to do or discover something

priests: people who lead prayers in a church

sinew: part of an animal connecting muscles and bones together

superstition: belief that is not based on fact

turpentine: mixture made from tree oil

Index